DOWNSIDE
OF DRUGS

Prescription
Painkillers

OxyContin®, Percocet®, Vicodin®, & Other Addictive Analgesics

DOWNSIDE OF DRUGS

DOWNSIDE OF DRUGS

Prescription Painkillers

OxyContin®, Percocet®, Vicodin®, & Other Addictive Analgesics

Rosa Waters

Mason Crest

Mason Crest
450 Parkway Drive, Suite D
Broomall, PA 19008
www.masoncrest.com

Printed and bound in the United States of America.

First printing
9 8 7 6 5 4 3 2 1

Series ISBN: 978-1-4222-3015-2
Hardcover ISBN: 978-1-4222-3026-8
Paperback ISBN: 978-1-4222-3194-4
ebook ISBN: 978-1-4222-8812-2

Cataloging-in-Publication Data on file with the Library of Congress.

Contents

INTRODUCTION

One of the best parts of getting older is the opportunity to make your own choices. As your parents give you more space and you spend more time with friends than family, you are called upon to make more decisions for yourself. Many important decisions that present themselves in the teen years may change your life. The people with whom you are friendly, how much effort you put into school and other activities, and what kinds of experiences you choose for yourself all affect the person you will become as you emerge from being a child into becoming a young adult.

One of the most important decisions you will make is whether or not you use substances like alcohol, marijuana, crystal meth, and cocaine. Even using prescription medicines incorrectly or relying on caffeine to get through your daily life can shape your life today and your future tomorrow. These decisions can impact all the other decisions you make. If you decide to say yes to drug abuse, the impact on your life is usually not a good one!

One suggestion I make to many of my patients is this: think about how you will respond to an offer to use drugs before it happens. In the heat of the moment, particularly if you're feeling some peer pressure, it can be hard to think clearly—so be prepared ahead of time. Thinking about why you don't want to use drugs and how you'll respond if you are asked to use them can make it easier to make a healthy decision when the time comes. Just like practicing a sport makes it easier to play in a big game, having thought about why drugs aren't a good fit for you and exactly what you might say to avoid them can give you the "practice" you need to do what's best for you. It can make a tough situation simpler once it arises.

In addition, talk about drugs with your parents or a trusted adult. This will both give you support and help you clarify your thinking. The decision is still yours to make, but adults can be a good resource. Take advantage of the information and help they can offer you.

Sometimes, young people fall into abusing drugs without really thinking about it ahead of time. It can sometimes be hard to recognize when you're making a decision that might hurt you. You might be with a friend or acquaintance in a situation that feels comfortable. There may be things in your life that are hard, and it could seem like using drugs might make them easier. It's also natural to be curious about new experiences. However, by not making a decision ahead of time, you may be actually making a decision without realizing it, one that will limit your choices in the future.

When someone offers you drugs, there is no flashing sign that says, "Hey, think about what you're doing!" Making a good decision may be harder because the "fun" part happens immediately while the downside—the damage to your brain and the rest of your body—may not be obvious right away. One of the biggest downsides of drugs is that they have long-term effects on your life. They could reduce your educational, career, and relationship opportunities. Drug use often leaves users with more problems than when they started.

Whenever you make a decision, it's important to know all the facts. When it comes to drugs, you'll need answers to questions like these: How do different drugs work? Is there any "safe" way to use drugs? How will drugs hurt my body and my brain? If I don't notice any bad effects right away, does that mean these drugs are safe? Are these drugs addictive? What are the legal consequences of using drugs? This book discusses these questions and helps give you the facts to make good decisions.

Reading this book is a great way to start, but if you still have questions, keep looking for the answers. There is a lot of information on the Internet, but not all of it is reliable. At the back of this book, you'll find a list of more books and good websites for finding out more about this drug. A good website is teens.drugabuse.gov, a site compiled for teens by the National Institute on Drug Abuse (NIDA). This is a reputable federal government agency that researches substance use and how to prevent it. This website does a good job looking at a lot of data and consolidating it into easy-to-understand messages.

What if you are worried you already have a problem with drugs? If that's the case, the best thing to do is talk to your doctor or another trusted adult to help figure out what to do next. They can help you find a place to get treatment.

Drugs have a downside—but as a young adult, you have the power to make decisions for yourself about what's best for you. Use your power wisely!

—Joshua Borus, MD

WHAT ARE PRESCRIPTION PAINKILLERS?

Prescription painkillers are powerful drugs that were created to help people who are in pain. When people have a serious illness or injury, painkillers can help them cope with the pain. Painkillers can help sick or injured people live their lives without being overwhelmed by pain.

All drugs are chemicals that in some way change the way the body works. Some drugs make the body function faster than normal. This type of drugs are known as stimulants. Other types of drugs slow the body, and these drugs are called depressants. Other types of drugs change how the body acts in other ways. Some drugs fight diseases.

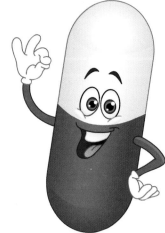

How much of a drug is taken also changes the effect it has on the body. Drugs can help human beings live healthier lives. We think of these types of drugs as medicines. But drugs can also be dangerous when they're not taken in the way they were intended to be used. When more than one kind of drug is taken at the same time, they can be even more dangerous. Even legal, helpful drugs can be deadly when they're not taken in the ways they are supposed to be used.

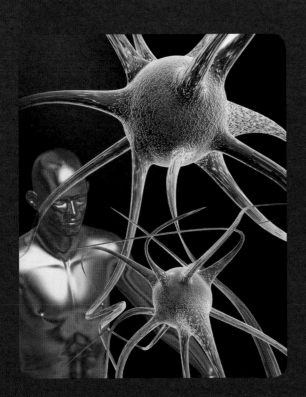

Painkillers interfere with the nervous system's *transmission* of the nerve signals the human body reads as pain. If the pain message doesn't get through the body's network of nerves, the body doesn't feel pain. These drugs do not get rid of the condition that causes pain. They don't make the body heal faster, and they don't fight germs. They only make the condition hurt less. No one likes to be in pain! But when painkillers are abused, they can be very dangerous. They have a very scary downside!

2. WHAT ARE THE DOWNSIDES OF THESE DRUGS?

Painkillers can be very addictive. This means that people can come to depend on them. They may feel as though they can't get through their lives without taking more and more of these drugs. Their bodies may truly need these drugs in order to function normally.

Drug addiction is like a trap. Once a person is caught in this trap, it's not easy to escape!

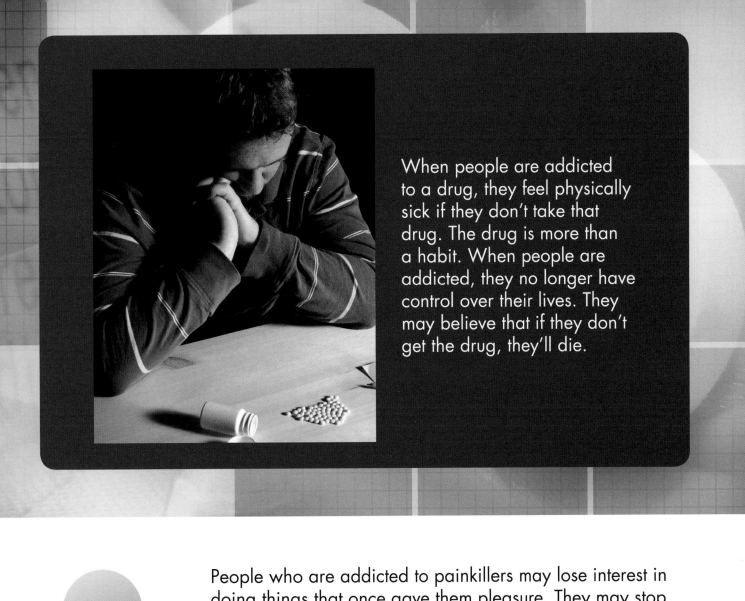

When people are addicted to a drug, they feel physically sick if they don't take that drug. The drug is more than a habit. When people are addicted, they no longer have control over their lives. They may believe that if they don't get the drug, they'll die.

People who are addicted to painkillers may lose interest in doing things that once gave them pleasure. They may stop hanging out with their friends. They may fail to live up to their responsibilities at school and work. Nothing seems interesting to them except getting more of their drug. Nothing else seems important. If their addiction goes on long enough, they may lose their friends. They may flunk out of school and lose their jobs. They can't escape their addiction without a lot of help.

And THAT's the downside to prescription painkillers!

3. WHAT ARE OPIOIDS?

The most powerful prescription painkillers are called opioids. This means they affect the body the same way that drugs do that come from opium. Opium comes from the seeds of a flower, the opium poppy. Some of the most commonly abused opioid pain-killers include OxyContin® and Vicodin®.

All opioids *stimulate* the parts of the brain that are connected with pleasure. This is why opioids produce a sense of well-being or even *euphoria*. Users want to experience that feeling again and again. They like the way their brains feel on the drug!

Opioids also affect brain regions that tell us what's important. So opioid users' ideas about what's important in their lives may change because of their drug use. They may no longer think their relationships with others are as important to them as getting high. They may no longer care about being kind—or even about having fun with their friends. They push their friends and family away. The only thing they care about is getting more of their drug.

Heroin is a very dangerous illegal drug that's made from opium. Users usually inject heroin with a needle. Heroin destroys lives—and painkillers have a lot in common with heroin!

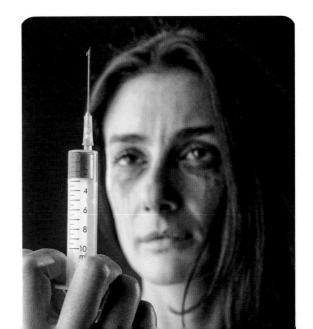

15

OxyContin is the *trade-marked* name for oxycodone. It's intended to help people handle *moderate* to *severe* pain. Oxycodone is one of the most dangerous prescription painkillers. It has the greatest potential for abuse—and it is as powerful as heroin. It affects the nervous system the same way heroin does.

NDC 59011-103-10

OxyContin® 20 mg
(oxycodone hydrochloride controlled-release) tablets

R$_x$ Only

100 Tablets

Co-promoted by
Purdue Pharma L.P. and
Abbott Laboratories

WY231 EXP JAN07.

OxyContin is taken as a pill. It looks like this.

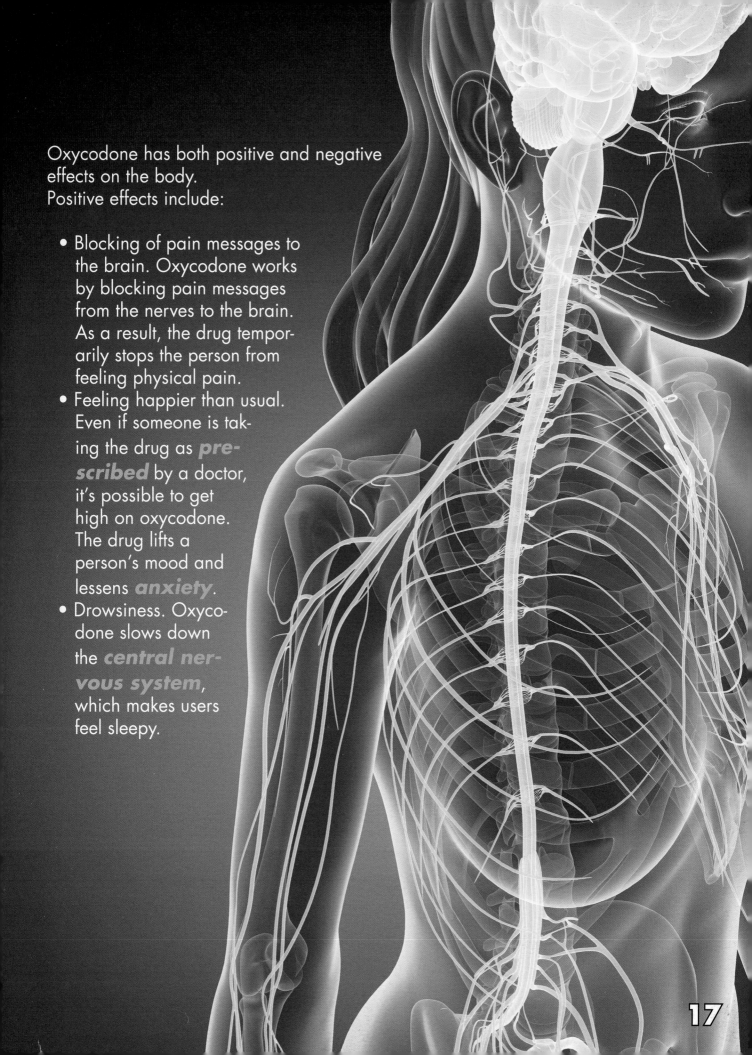

Oxycodone has both positive and negative effects on the body.
Positive effects include:

- Blocking of pain messages to the brain. Oxycodone works by blocking pain messages from the nerves to the brain. As a result, the drug temporarily stops the person from feeling physical pain.
- Feeling happier than usual. Even if someone is taking the drug as **prescribed** by a doctor, it's possible to get high on oxycodone. The drug lifts a person's mood and lessens **anxiety**.
- Drowsiness. Oxycodone slows down the **central nervous system**, which makes users feel sleepy.

17

5. WHAT IS PERCOCET®?

Percocet contains oxycodone along with acetaminophen. (Acetaminophen is another painkiller. It's often sold under the trademarked name Tylenol. You don't need a prescription to buy acetaminophen by itself.) Because Percocet contains oxycodone, it can be just as dangerous as OxyContin.

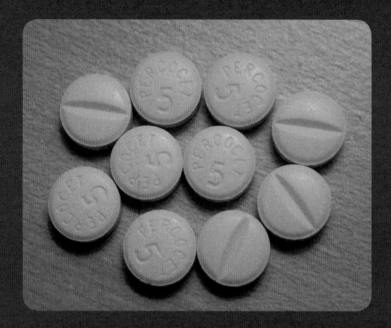

Oxycodone is sold under many other trademarked names. These include:

- Percodan
- Roxiprin
- Roxicet
- Endodan
- Endocet

The negative side effects of oxycodone are shown on the diagram on the next page. In addition to these unpleasant side effects, some people are allergic to oxycodone. Signs of an allergic reaction include a rash around the mouth, tightening of the throat, or swelling of the throat and mouth. If someone taking oxycodone has these symptoms, she should stop taking the drug and get medical assistance right away.

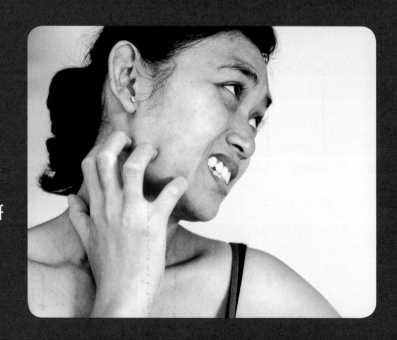

Side effects of
Oxycodone

Red color - more serious effect

Central:
- Hallucination
- Confusion
- Fainting
- Dizziness
- Loss of appetite
- Lightheadedness
- Drowsiness
- Headache
- Mood changes

Mouth, tongue or lips:
- Swelling
- Dryness

Eyes:
- Swelling
- Smaller pupil
- Redness

Face:
- Swelling

Throat:
- Hoarseness
- Swelling
- Difficulty swallowing

Skin:
- Hives
- Rash
- Flushing
- Sweating
- Itching

Respiratory:
- Difficulty breathing
- Slowed breathing

Heart:
- Fast or slow heartbeat

Muscular:
- Seizures
- Weakness

Gastric:
- Nausea
- Vomiting

Intestinal:
- Constipation

Hands, feet, ankles, or lower legs: - Swelling

6. WHAT IS VICODIN®?

Vicodin is the trademarked name for another prescription painkiller that contains a combination of drugs. It's used to treat moderate to severe pain, and sometimes it's also prescribed to treat cough. Vicodin contains acetaminophen, but its most dangerous ingredient is a chemical called hydrocodone. Hydrocodone isn't as powerful as oxycodone, but it's still dangerous.

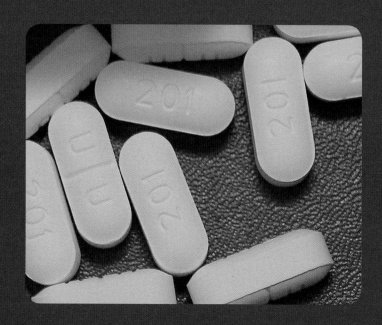

Hydrocodone is available as tablets, capsules and syrups. Some of its other trademarked names include:

- Anexsia
- Hycodan
- Lorcet
- Norco
- Dicodid
- Hycomine
- Lortab
- Tussionex

Side effects of
Vicodin

Red = more serious

Psychological
- Anxiousness
- Dizziness
- Drowsiness
- Headache
- Mood Changes
- Fainting
- Confusion
- Fear
- Unusual thoughts or behavior
- Loss of appetite

Ears
- Ringing sound

Throat
- Swelling

Eyes
- Blurred Vision
- Yellowing

Face, lips, or tongue
- Dryness
- Swelling

Muscular
- Seizures

Heart
- Slowed heart rate

Stomach
- Nausea
- Vomiting
- Distress
- Pain

Skin
- Hives
- Itching
- Yellowing

Lungs
- Difficulty breathing
- Shallow breathing

Intestinal
- Constipation
- Clay-colored stools

Urinary
- Problems urinating
- Dark urine

21

7. WHAT ARE SOME OF THE OTHER DANGEROUS PRESCRIPTION PAINKILLERS?

Meperidine (brand name Demerol), hydromorphone (brand name Dilaudid), and propoxyphene (brand name Darvon) are three other dangerous and addictive painkillers. They are sold as pills, but people who abuse them sometimes crush them and then smoke them, snort them into their noses, or inject them into their blood with needles. These three drugs are among the top-ten drugs reported in drug-abuse deaths in the United States. Some European countries have made these drugs illegal, but in America, they are still legally prescribed.

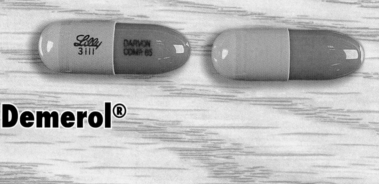

Demerol®

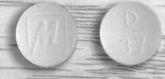

Dilaudid®

Dilaudid is often called "drug store heroin" on the streets.

Darvon®

Another drug called methadone is used in addiction treatment centers to help people handle withdrawal symptoms from heroin and other drugs. It is also prescribed as a pain-killer. It can be taken as a tablet or a syrup. Even though methadone is used to treat addiction, people can become addicted to this drug too — and it has dangerous side effects. Overdoses from methadone caused 785 deaths in just one year in the state of Florida alone.

8. WHAT HAPPENS TO YOUR BODY WHEN YOU USE PAINKILLERS?

Painkillers don't cure diseases. They can only mask the pain for which they are taken. When someone is continuously trying to dull pain, he may find himself taking higher and higher doses—and eventually discover that he cannot make it through the day without the drug. Now he's addicted.

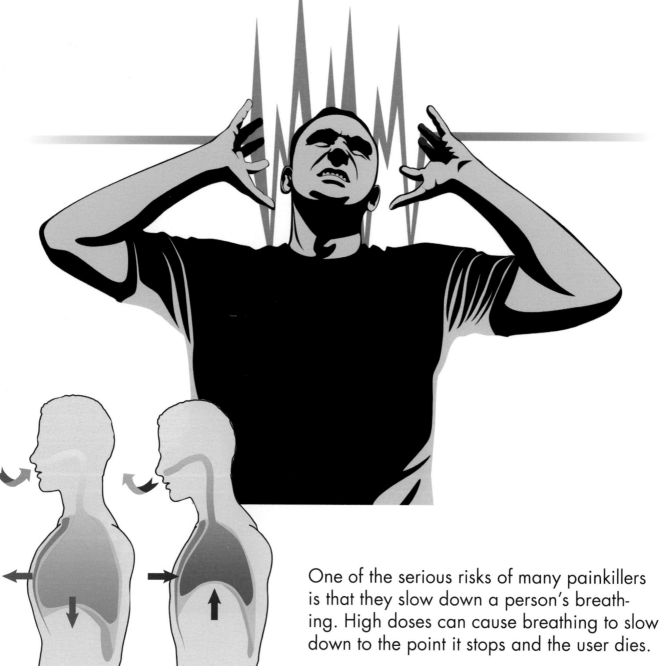

One of the serious risks of many painkillers is that they slow down a person's breathing. High doses can cause breathing to slow down to the point it stops and the user dies.

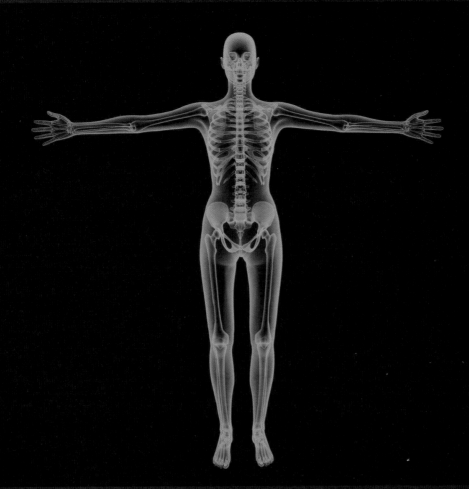

Painkillers can also have these effects on users' bodies:

- constipation (difficulty having a bowel movement)
- nausea and vomiting
- dizziness
- increased risk of heart attack
- *coma*
- death

When someone who is addicted to painkillers tries to quit, she may have these symptoms:

- muscle and bone pain
- *insomnia*
- diarrhea
- vomiting
- cold flashes with goose bumps
- *involuntary* leg movements

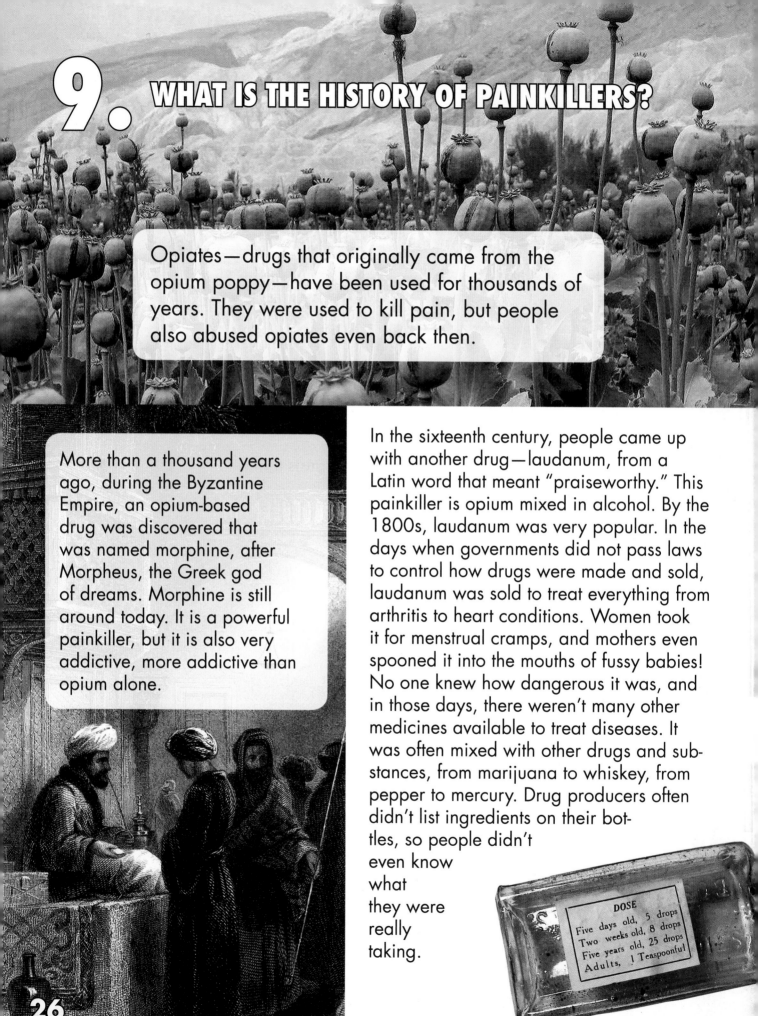

Opiates—drugs that originally came from the opium poppy—have been used for thousands of years. They were used to kill pain, but people also abused opiates even back then.

More than a thousand years ago, during the Byzantine Empire, an opium-based drug was discovered that was named morphine, after Morpheus, the Greek god of dreams. Morphine is still around today. It is a powerful painkiller, but it is also very addictive, more addictive than opium alone.

In the sixteenth century, people came up with another drug—laudanum, from a Latin word that meant "praiseworthy." This painkiller is opium mixed in alcohol. By the 1800s, laudanum was very popular. In the days when governments did not pass laws to control how drugs were made and sold, laudanum was sold to treat everything from arthritis to heart conditions. Women took it for menstrual cramps, and mothers even spooned it into the mouths of fussy babies! No one knew how dangerous it was, and in those days, there weren't many other medicines available to treat diseases. It was often mixed with other drugs and substances, from marijuana to whiskey, from pepper to mercury. Drug producers often didn't list ingredients on their bottles, so people didn't even know what they were really taking.

DOSE
Five days old, 5 drops
Two weeks old, 8 drops
Five years old, 25 drops
Adults, 1 Teaspoonful

A few years later, when the American Civil War broke out, morphine was used as a painkiller for wounded soldiers. Many men became addicted.

Throughout the early nineteenth century, the recreational use of opium grew. In Europe, many people smoked it in places called "opium dens." Opium even caused wars. When China tried to stop opium from being shipped out of its ports, the British sent warships to get the opium people craved!

In 1874, chemists trying to find a less addictive form of morphine made heroin. It was sold by the Bayer drug company, which today sells aspirin, a much safer painkiller. Heroin had twice the power of morphine, and heroin addiction soon became a serious problem.

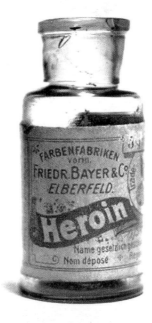

U.S Food and Drug Administration

The U.S. Congress banned opium in 1905, and the next year passed the Pure Food and Drug Act that required contents labeling on all medicines. Nowadays, most countries have organizations that control the sale and production of drugs. In the United States, the Food and Drug Administration has this job.

27

10. WHY ARE SOME PAINKILLERS ADDICTIVE?

Our brains are built to experience pleasure in ways that help human beings survive. Each time we perform certain activities—like finding and eating food, drinking water, having sex, and caring for children—our brains give us a reward. The reward systems in our brains release a chemical called dopamine. Dopamine is a kind of neurotransmitter. It helps carry messages between the nerve cells in our brains. When dopamine gets released, it feels good. We like the feeling, so we want to repeat the activity that made us feel that way. Painkillers mess up the system, though. These drugs flood the brain with dopamine.

Dopamine is what gives people a "rush"—what makes them feel "high"—when they take painkillers.

When a person becomes addicted to painkillers, his brain's reward system thinks that these drugs are as necessary as food and water. The brain thinks it can't survive without the chemicals in the painkillers. Dr. House, on the TV show *House M.D.*, is a fictional example of someone who cannot function without taking painkillers.

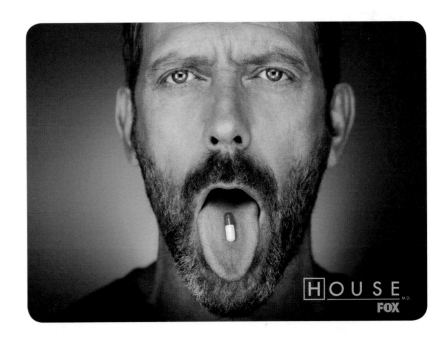

11. WHAT DO PAINKILLERS DO TO YOUR BRAIN?

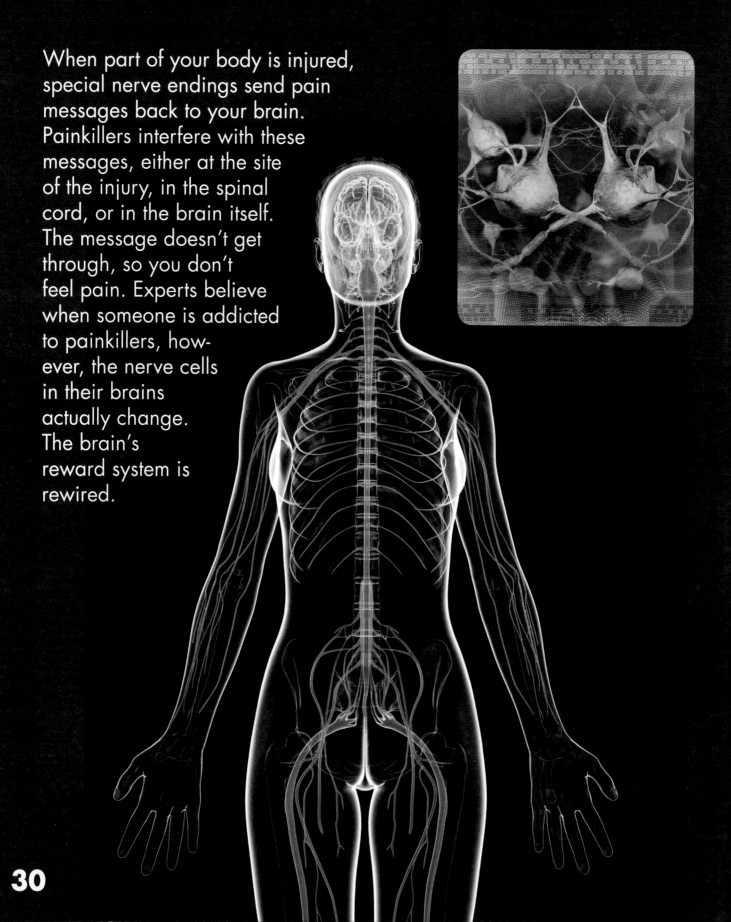

When part of your body is injured, special nerve endings send pain messages back to your brain. Painkillers interfere with these messages, either at the site of the injury, in the spinal cord, or in the brain itself. The message doesn't get through, so you don't feel pain. Experts believe when someone is addicted to painkillers, however, the nerve cells in their brains actually change. The brain's reward system is rewired.

The brain responds to the presence of the pain medicine by increasing the number of receptors for the drug. The brain's nerve cells are no longer functioning normally. Instead of looking for other kinds of pleasure-producing triggers, the brain responds only to the pleasure produced by the drug. Eating, drinking, and even sex no longer seem as pleasurable as getting high.

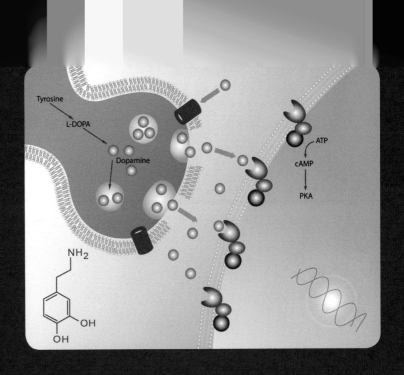

On top of that, painkillers stop the body from producing its natural painkillers. Endorphins are a chemical that the body normally makes that helps us cope with pain. People who are addicted to painkillers no longer produce as many endorphins. This means that without the drug, their pain may be unbearable.

DO TEENAGERS ABUSE PAINKILLERS?

More and more young adults are abusing painkillers. In fact, teen drug abuse with prescription painkillers is now second only to marijuana in popularity.

Here are some scary numbers from recent surveys of teenagers:

- One in 10 high school seniors reported abusing prescription painkillers in 2012.
- Almost 50 percent of teens believe that taking prescription drugs is much safer than using illegal street drugs. (They're wrong!)
- Five times as many high school seniors are using painkillers to get high as use meth.
- According to a 2012 report from the U.S. Centers for Disease Control and Prevention, fatal overdoses of prescription painkillers are the main reason why accidental poisoning deaths among teens ages 15 through 19 years skyrocketed by 91 percent between 2000 and 2009.
- Every day in the United States, 2,500 young people between the ages of 12 and 17 abuse a prescription pain reliever for the first time.
- More than 60 percent of teenagers who abuse painkillers get them from their home medicine cabinets.

Why are so many teenagers abusing painkillers? Here are some of the reasons young people have given:

- to fit in with their friends who are getting high on painkillers
- to escape from problems
- to relax
- to relieve boredom
- to seem grown up
- to rebel
- to try something new; to experiment

Young people who abuse painkillers think the drugs are a solution to some situation they are facing—but eventually, the drugs become the problem. The consequences of abusing painkillers are always worse than the problems the teens started out with.

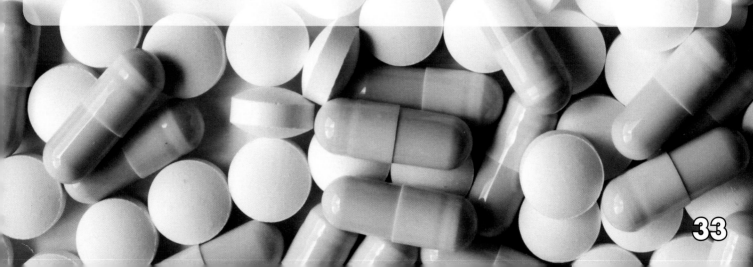

13. HOW CAN YOU TELL IF SOMEONE IS BECOMING ADDICTED TO PAINKILLERS?

Here are ten warning signs to watch for if you think someone you know may be experiencing a dependency on these drugs:

1. Usage increase. People who are addicted need to take more and more of the drug in order to get the same effects.

2. Change in personality. People who are addicted will have changes in their energy levels, their moods, and their ability to concentrate.

3. Social withdrawal. People who are addicted will no longer be interested in spending time with family and friends.

4. Ongoing use. People who are addicted will continue to use painkillers even after the medical condition for which the drugs were prescribed has improved.

5. A lot of time and trouble spent on obtaining prescriptions. People who are addicted are willing to drive great distances to faraway pharmacies and visit multiple doctors to obtain the drugs, all so that no one will be alerted to their problem.

6. Change in daily habits and appearance. People who are addicted will no longer care about personal hygiene. Their sleeping and eating habits may change. They may have a constant cough, a runny nose, and red, glazed eyes.

7. Neglect of responsibilities. People who are addicted will often forget to do household chores and pay bills. They may call in sick to school or work more often.

8. Increased sensitivity. Normal sights, sounds, and emotions may seem too much to handle for a person who is addicted.

9. Blackouts and forgetfulness. People with an addiction may forget events that have taken place. They may experience blackouts where they can't recall what they were doing.

10. Defensiveness. People who are addicted may become defensive and lash out in response to simple questions when they are trying to hide their addiction.

14. ARE PAINKILLERS AND CRIME CONNECTED?

Because painkillers affect the nervous system the same way heroin does, some users are turning to painkillers instead of illegal street drugs. Armed robberies of pharmacies have taken place where the robbers demanded painkillers instead of cash.

Painkiller addicts sometimes break into the homes of sick or elderly people in order to raid their medicine cabinets.

OxyContin, widely known as "hillbilly heroin" because of its abuse in the Appalachian region, has become a major crime problem in this part of the United States. In one county, it was estimated that addiction to this drug was behind 80 percent of the crime.

15. WHAT HAPPENS IF YOU MIX ALCOHOL AND PAINKILLERS?

Combining even a single drink—a beer or a glass of wine—with pain-killers can be very dangerous. Alcohol has some of the same effects on the brain and body as painkillers do. When taken together, the effects of each is even stronger than usual. The result can be deadly.

If you drink alcohol at the same time you're taking a prescription painkiller, here's what could happen:

- You could become too drowsy to drive, walk, or talk.
- Your blood pressure could drop to a dangerously low level.
- You might not be able to think clearly enough to make good decisions.
- Your breathing could slow down—to the point that you might die.

What should I do if I think someone has overdosed on painkillers?

An overdose is when someone takes too much of any drug or medication, so that it causes serious, harmful symptoms or even death. If you think you or someone else has overdosed on a drug, you should always call 911 immediately. If it's not an emergency but you have questions about preventing an overdose, you can also call the National Poison Control Center (1-800-222-1222) from anywhere in the United States. It is a free call and it's *confidential*. You can call for any reason, 24/7.

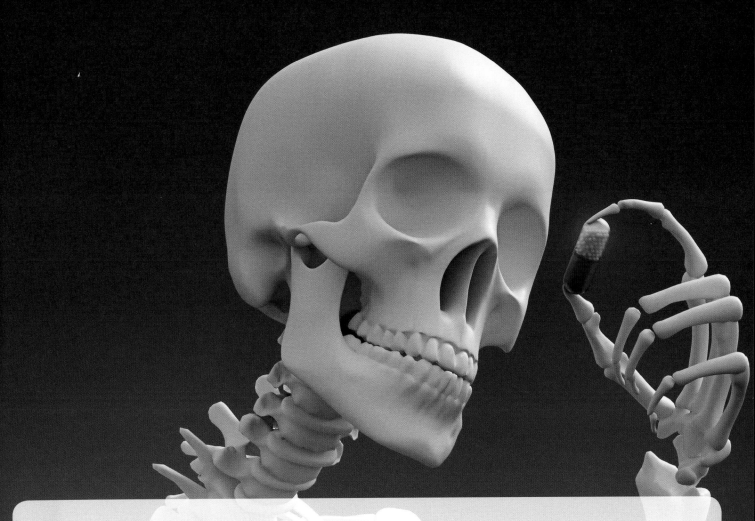

Can I use painkillers and stay safe?

Not everyone is likely to get addicted to painkillers. Some people don't get the rush of euphoria from taking these drugs that other people do. According to medical experts, though, about 5 to 10 percent of the population have brains that are "wired" for addiction to painkillers.

How can you know if you're one of that fraction of people? You can't. There's no test to tell you. So the smart thing is to not put yourself in the position where you might get addicted. That doesn't mean you should never take painkillers when you're in pain. Studies have shown that when these drugs are taken exactly as doctors prescribe them, they are safe, they manage pain effectively, and they rarely cause addiction. When a person begins to experience signs of prescription pain medication abuse, he can avoid drug addiction by stopping use completely.

If you think you might already be addicted, let your doctor know. She can tell you how to get the help you need.

FURTHER READING

Adams, Taite. *Opiate Addiction: The Painkiller Addiction Epidemic, Heroin Addiction, and the Way Out.* Petersburg, Fla.: Rapid Response Press, 2013.

Colvin, Rod. *Overcoming Prescription Drug Addiction: A Guide to Coping and Understanding.* Madison, N.J.: Atticus, 2008.

Fletcher, Anne M. *Inside Rehab: The Surprising Truth About Addiction Treatment—and How to Get Help That Works.* New York: Viking, 2013.

Lyon, Joshua. *Pill Head: The Secret Life of a Painkiller Addict.* New York: Hyperion, 2010.

Pinksky, Drew. *When Painkillers Become Dangerous: What Everyone Needs to Know About Oxycontin and Other Prescription Drugs.* Center City, Minn.: Hazelden, 2004.

Seppala, Marvin D. *Prescription Painkillers: History, Pharmacology, and Treatment.* Center City, Minn.: Hazelden, 2010.

Sheff, David. *Clean: Overcoming Addiction and Ending America's Greatest Tragedy.* New York: Houghton Mifflin Harcourt, 2013.

FIND OUT MORE ON THE INTERNET

CDC: Preventing Prescription Painkiller Overdoses
www.cdc.gov/injury/about/focus-rx.html

Drug Facts: Prescription Drugs
www.abovetheinfluence.com/facts/drugspresciptionrx

Prescription for Addiction
online.wsj.com/news/articles/SB10000872396390444223104578036933277566700?mg=reno64-wsj&url=http%3A%2F%2Fonline.wsj.com%2Farticle%2FSB10000872396390444223104578036933277566700.html

Prescription Pain Medication Addiction and Abuse: 7 Myths
www.webmd.com/pain-management/features/prescription-painkiller-addiction-7-myths

Prescription Pain Meds
www.drugfreeworld.org

Science Daily: Teens Increasingly Abuse Prescription Painkillers
www.sciencedaily.com/releases/2012/11/121130151136.htm

U.S. News & World Report: Teens and Prescription Painkillers
health.usnews.com/health-news/news/articles/2013/10/31/one-in-10-teens-has-misused-prescription-painkillers-survey

GLOSSARY

anxiety: A feeling of nervousness or worry.

central nervous system: The brain and the spinal cord, which together control most of the processes in your body.

coma: A deep unconsciousness that you can't wake up from.

confidential: Kept a secret, such as between a doctor and her patient.

euphoria: An intense feeling of excitement or happiness.

insomnia: A condition where a person is unable to fall asleep or has trouble staying asleep.

involuntary: Outside of your control.

moderate: An average amount; not too much or too little.

prescribed: Told by a doctor to take a certain drug or undergo a certain treatment.

severe: Very serious.

stimulate: Raise levels of activity in a certain part of your body.

trademarked: Registered with the government, so no one else can sell a product under that name.

transmission: The process of carrying or broadcasting a signal.

INDEX

PICTURE CREDITS

ABOUT THE AUTHOR
AND THE CONSULTANT

ROSA WATERS lives in New York State. She has worked as a writer for several years, producing works on health, history, and other topics.

DR. JOSHUA BORUS, MD, MPH, graduated from the Harvard Medical School and the Harvard School of Public Health. He completed a residency in pediatrics and then served as chief resident at Floating Hospital for Children at Tufts Medical Center before completing a fellowship in Adolescent Medicine at Boston Children's Hospital. He is currently an attending physician in the Division of Adolescent and Young Adult Medicine at Boston Children's Hospital and an instructor of pediatrics at Harvard Medical School.